ابن عربي

IBN 'ARABI

THE GREAT MUSLIM THINKER OF MYSTICISM

S.A.Q HUSAINI

Qadeem Press Edition
Breathing Life into Forgotten Pages
www.qadeempress.com

Find our titles on your favourite online bookstore using the keyword 'Qadeem Press'

TO
THE DEAR MEMORY OF
MY BELOVED SISTER
SALMAH

My heart is capable of every form:
A cloister for the monk, a fane for idols,
A pasture for gazellers, the vatary's Ka'ba,
The tables of the Torah, the Quran.
Love is the creed I hold
wherever turn his camels,
Love is still my creed and faith.

IBNE 'ARABI

CONTENTS

PREFACE

One Friday, in 1928, one of my Arabic masters enquired of me: "Shaikh al-Akbar writes that if he had not written the *Futūhāt al-Makkiyya,* he would have been set on fire. How could he has been so set on fire?"

This question made me highly inquisitive about the Shaikh; and I took the earliest opportunity to study him.

The following statement by E. G. Browne in his *Literary History of Persia,* (p 500), added strength to my resolve: "So far as I am aware, no adequate study of his works and doctrines have yet been made in Europe though few fields of greater promise offer themselves to the aspiring Arabist who is interested in this characteristic aspect of Eastern thought,"

After making a fair study of his representative works the problem was what to do and on what topic to concentrate. A complete analysis of his works would take a long time; and as far as I know there is not even a biography of the Great Shaikh in English which can be called satisfactory.

So in this small volume I have confined myself to a detailed biography of the Shaikh, a short account of his works, translation of some of his valuable sayings and of his views in brief on a few topics.

The biographical portion of this work has been directly translated from *Nafh ut-Tib* of al-Maqqari (which contains the best extant biography of the Shaikh), *Shadhrat al-Dhahab* of Abü al-Faläh Abd al-Hayy (the Arabic text of which is published in the *Journal of the Royal Asiatic Society* in 1906). and the biographical note attached to the *Futühät al-Makkiyya.* I have also consulted the book called *Wisdom of the Prophets* by Khaja Khan which contains a short note on the life of the Shaikh, and used the article in the *Encyclopaedia of Islam* for fixing certain dates. Besides, I have derived what help I could get from Browne's *Literary History of Persia* and Clement Huart's *History of Arabic, Literature.*

The sayings of the Shaikh have been translated from the *Shadhrat al Dhahab* with some help from Nicholson's work. The short notes on the views of the Shaikh on certain topics were gathered by me from both the *Futuhat al-Makkiyya* and the *Fusus.* I have derived much help from Nicholson's Notes on the *Fusus* in determining the Shaikh's views on God.

His views on a few topics have been laboriously

collected by me from the original works of the Shaikh. My indebtedness to the European authors is only to the extent of their valuable remarks and suggestions. Besides, it must be admitted that, but for Nicholson's endeavours, the Arabic text of *Shadhrat al-Dhahab* would not have been available to me. Moreover, Nicholson's *Notes on Fusus al-Hikam,* and Khaja Khan's *Wisdom of the Prophets* have helped me for a good deal in making a scientific study of the *Fusus.*

As far as the biographical portion of this book is concerned nothing can be added to it unless some new manuscripts containing the life of the Great Shaikh are discovered. As for the other portions, they are fruits gathered by hand cast at random. Some of the best fruits may have escaped.

Yet to the best of my knowledge, this will be the first concise book on Ibne-'Arabi giving all the particulars that may be required by a casual reader interested in him.

The materials are very abstruse and unyielding, and sweeping remarks and the Great Shaikh risky and bazardous. I am perfectly aware of my shortcomings and ill-providedness and send this book to the press with much diffidence and anxious prayers.

S.A.Q. HUSAINI

CHAPTER I

EARLY LIFE OF THE SHAIKH IN SPAIN

Shaikh al Akbar Muhiyuddin Ibne 'Arabi alias Muhammad, son of 'Ali, son of Muhammad al 'Arabi, son of Ahmad, son of Ardallah, the Hatimite, was a descendant of the famous Hatim Ta'i, the world renowned benefactor whose liberality and generosity are even now proverbial throughout the Islamic world and its surroundings. After the conquest of Spain by the Arabs, the ancestors of Ibne Arabi came and settled in Spain. Of all the writers Ibne Abbar is quite solitary in suggesting that Ibne 'Arabi was a Marian and that his father was a carpenter who lived at Seville till 597 A.H.

He was known in the West as Ibne 'Arabi and in Spain as Ibn Suraqa. But in the East he was generally known as Ibne 'Arabi without the definite article "al" to differentiate between him and Abu Bakr, the Qadi of Seville who was also called Ibne 'Arabi.

It seems that 'Ali, the father of Ibne 'Arabi, was childless for a long time; and a story has it, that he met Muhiyuddin Abdul Qadir Jilani and requested him to pray to Allah to bestow on him a male child. Accordingly, the great saint of Jilan, who was very near the end of his life, prayed for a son and bade 'Ali name the child Muhiyuddin after him. It is also said that the great saint blessed the prospective child in a special way and prophesied that the child would be the master of all Divine secrets.

Be that as it may, the illustrious son of 'Ali was born at Mursya (Murcia), the beautiful city of parks and gardens, built by the Arabs in Spain, on the night preceding Monday, the 17th of Ramdan, 560 A.H (July 29, 1165 A.C.).

The almightly was highly bountiful to the new-born child and endowed him with all the good qualities of both heart and mind. His father seems to have been in affluent circumstances and gave his darling child the best education available thereabout. 'Ali, the father of the Shaikh, also seems to have been a good scholar and he spared no pains to give his boy a sound education in his early days.

When the Shaikh was a boy of eight, *i.e.* in 568 A.H. (1173 A.C.), his father took him to Seville for his education. In that town the boy studied the Qur'an and *Al-Kafi* under Abu Bakr bin Khalaf. He studied *Hadith* (traditions of the prophet) under Ibn Muallif Abu al-Hasan Sharih, son of Muhammad, son of Sharih al Ruaini; and *Fikh* (jurisprudence) under Abu Al-Qasim Al-Sharrat of Cordova. The Sheikh's family belonged to the school of Imam Malik in religion.

He also attended the classes of Abu Bakr Muhammad, son of Abu Jamra, to study *Kitab ut Taisri*. Likewise he attended the classes of Ibn Zarqun and Abu Muhammad 'Abd al-Haq al-Azdi of Seville and a horde of others of the East and the West.

He was permitted to narrate *Hadith* by a great body of scholars among whom were al-Hafizal-Salafi, Ibn al-Asakir, Abul Faraj and Ibn al-Jawzi.

The young boy from Murcia was intelligent, brisk and quick to grasp. Even as a student, he was head and shoulders above others. Besides all the good qualities of the mind, he was highly devotional, sincere and honest. His character was spotless and reputation unstained. His avarice for knowledge knew no bounds and was always keen after the naked truth. He was hardworking, painstaking and showed leanings towards a life of hard penance, renunciation and poverty.

Even as a student, he became famous, and people came from far and near to meet him. He always spent his spare time with Sufis and *Ahl al-Haq* (People of

Reality). His mastery over the language was perfect, his vocabulary immense. He was writing very fine and eloquent poetry, and his prose too became famous throughout the land.

Dhahabi writes of him: "His vocabulary was very vast and his sparkling intelligence, splendid memory and dazzling mental force are replendently displayed by his complete mastery over the details of the problems of Sufism, his innumerable compilations of *'Irfan* (gnosis), illumination, etc. When he sang, he fell into a sort of swoon and it appeared as if he was drunk."

The young boy, when grown to man-hood, began to display signs of prophetic greatness, and almost all those qualities that are essential for a prophet (ofcourse, except revelation). A clear and unsoiled heart he owned. An imagination of a supreme sort he possessed. All those psychic qualities of dreams, telepathy, psychometry, television and chairvoyance that are indispensable for prophethood began to manifest themselves in the young man so much that to his acquired knowledge the youth was adding knowledge through sources which are not available to the ordinary students. As appears from Dhahabi's account, he was having the prophetic trance also.

A very important element of prophethood is dream. Not only our young scholar had extraordinary dreams, but he was a strong believer in them, their utility and utilisation. Ibn Shawdakin writes that he used to say: "A man must endeavour to have presence of mind in dreams so that he may be the master of his thoughts, which he has gathered as a result of reasoning, even in sleep as in waking. If a man gets this presence of mind and makes it become a part of his habit he will get its fruit in the *barzakh* (the intermediate world) and be highly benefited by it. Every man must strive to attain this habit, for Allah willing, it will be of great use."

The prophetic qualities began to manifest themselves, and the promising young lad gave out that he had received the *Khirqa* or emblem of discipleship from Khidr (the living prophet of Allah).

Al Qutb al-'Unaini writes in his book *Mir 'at al-Zaman* that Ibne 'Arabi used to say that he knew *Ism al-A 'zam* (the great name of Allah) and that he knew Alchemy not by acquisition but through supernatural sources.

He visited Maria in 595 A.H. and it is there that he wrote his famous book *Mawaqi' al-Nujum.*

In 597, the Shaikh, now about thirty-seven years old, entered Jaya (Ceuta). He met Abu 'Abdallah al-'Arabi and a host of other scholars. The Shaikh writes: "When I was in Ceuta, I dreamt that I was wedded to all the stars of the sky. There was not a single star left, and I married every one of them with great spiritual pleasure. Then I married the moons. I mentioned this dream to a friend who consulted a famous scholar and interpreter. He glorified the dream and said: 'Immeasurable bounty is coming upon tbe dreamer. Knowledge from above will dawn on him, and the secrets and specialities of all the stars will be combined in him in such a way that he shall have no compeer among his contemporaries.' He was silent for some time and then said: 'If the dreamer is in this city, it must be that Spanish young man who has arrived in it.'" The last, sentence shows that Shaikh Ibne 'Arabi was already growing famous throughout the land as a brilliant scholar, famous writer of elegent poetry and beautiful prose, as a Sufi of great repute and last not least, of all as a great occultist and promising spiritualist.

The Shaikh served under an old lady saint, by name Fatima bint al-Waliyyah, who was ninety-five years of age but hale and hearty and who was said to have had the sight of Allah in everything in the world.

These are the particulars that are available about the early life of the Great Saint. By the time he left Spain, his college career was practically over, he had earned a name as a scholar of rare eminence and writer of great brilliance. His fame reached far and wide, and princes invited him to be their secretary. He acted as secretary to some prince, and then, resigning his post, took up a life of renunciation and poverty in 598 (1202 A.C.).

He left Spain in the same year for Africa, and visited some of the cities of Northern Africa till he reached Egypt. Thence he went to the Hijaz, Baghdad, Mosul, Aleppo and other places till he finally settled down at Damascus. Spain was left once for all, and the Great Shaikh never returned to it.

CHAPTER II

THE WANDERINGS OF THE SHAIKH

In 598 (1202 A.C.) the Shaikh left Seville for the East. Travel and adventure are the handmaids of success, and the young adventurer prospered a good deal after he left his native land. He had already visited Tunis in 590 (1194 A.C.) and this time his first landing place after leaving Spain is not exactly known. But all reports agree that he left Spain only with the intention of performing the Hajj pilgrimage.

I have already observed that the promising young scholar was evincing signs of prophetic tendencies and that he was fond of all holy practices. He was specially bent upon visiting tombs and spending days near them. It is his love of visiting the holy places and probably a sense of duty of performing the Hajj that made Ibne 'Arabi leave for Makkah.

Though the exact town of his first visit after leaving Seville is not known, he did not go to Makkah direct. He landed in Egypt and spent a year or two in that land

and its surroundings. During this stay, his fame immensely increased and it seems that the Shaikh, fresh from his studies and knowledge of realities, was a bit incautious in his pronouncements. This naturally resulted in a serious opposition on the part of the orthodox; and the Great Shaikh was even arrested and released. He was forced to leave the land and his immense following in search of a safe and calmer atmosphere. The fire kindled by him in Egypt did not extinguish. The orthodox raved at his heretical utterances and could detect heresy and monistic tendencies very easily even in his later savings, in spite of the fact that his later sayings of any significance were closely interwoven with popular beliefs and mythology of a highly imaginative character.

No pains were spared by his opponents like Ibn al-Taimia, al-Taftazani and Ibrahim al-Biqa'i in denouncing him a heretic and a monist. The orthodox Egypt was up in arms against him. The heterodox and some of the simple minded citizens hailed him to heavens. He was considered a *Siddiq* by his adherents to rhyme with the word *Zindiq* which was freely applied to him by his deadly opponents. We also understand that there was a very strong movement in Egypt to assassinate him.

It was during the ramblings of Ibne 'Arabi that he met for the first time his favourite disciple Sadruddin of Qonia. A horseman met a pedestrian coming from the opposite direction. The pedestrian accosted the horseman thus: "Whence do you come? Whither would you go ? What have you to obtain on the road ?" The rider immediately replied: "From knowledge to the substance, to attain both the ends." The horseman was Shaikh Muhiyuddin Ibne 'Arabi and the pedestrian Sadruddin who then met him for the first time. Since this first meeting, Sadruddin became a disciple of the Great Shaikh and he is considered to be greatest in that capacity.

Shaikh Shahabuddin Suhrawardi, Naj-muddin Razi' Muslihuddin Sadi, Abu'al-Hasan al-Maghribi al-Shdadhuli, Jalaluddin Rumi, Shaikh 'Umar bin al-Farid and Ibn al-Jawzi were some of the illustrious savants who were his contemporaries; and we know that he met Ibn al-Jawzi, Suhrawardi, Ibn al-Farid and others.

He got the permission of Ibn al-Jawzi to succeed him in his work of reporting *Hadith.* After writing his *Futuhat al-Makkiyya,* he wrote to Ibn al-Farid seeking his permission to write a commentary on his *Ta'ia.* The author replied: "Your work, *Futuhat al-Makkiyya,* is a sufficient commentary for my *Ta'ia.*"

Abdallah bin Sa'd al-Yafa'i writes in his *Irshad* that Shaikh met Shahabuddin Suhrawardi, each looked at the other for a time and then they parted without saying anything. After this meeting, Ibne 'Arabi was asked his opinion of Suhrawardi. He said: "From horn to heel is saturated with the *sunnah* — the path of Muhammad(Peace be upon him)."

Suhrawardi, when questioned similarly, said: "Muhiyuddin is an ocean of *haqaiq* (realities)"

He paid a short visit to Baghdad in 601 A. H. and remained there for twelve days. He was fascinated by the path of the People of Reality. He was also growing famous by this time for his inspirations, dreams, penance and battle with the *nafs,* and was considered to be the most prominent living saint throughout Hijaz and Syria. After his short stay of twelve days at Baghdad he went to Makkah, remained there for about seven years and came back to Baghdad in 608 A.H.(1211-12 A.C.). He remained in Baghdad for some time and travelled throughout Mesopotamia and Syria. He visited Mosul and came back to Makkah in 611 A.H. (1214-15 A.C.). By this time his fame had reached far and wide. Noted scholars and Sufis of great repute sought his audience and came from distant lands to have his blessings and learn from him truths of the upper world and the realities of this lower, one. He became famous as a Sufi of high order, a composer of elegant mystic hemistitches and a writer of immense volumes on the most abstruse and difficult subjects. His fame for innovation in style, language and method of presenting the most shocking truths clad in popular beliefs and Islamic mythology spread like wild-fire; and kings and princes longed for his blessings and company.

He had an immense following of scholars, nobles and ordinary men. His vast knowledge and deep insight into the character and nature of human souls enabled him to talk to men of all shades of opinions in their own diction. He was admired everywhere for his marvellous character, peaceful intentions, broad toleration, catholic outlook on life, his immense piety, wonderful scholarship and deep insight into the realities of existence.

CHAPTER III

AT MAKKAH

The Great Shaikh arrived at Makkah in *601* A.H. and lived there for a long period. It was after performing the pilgrimage of the Hajj that he thought of writing a systematic treatise on religious matters. He must have been planning to write such a treatise for a long time; and Makkah, its holiness, its surroundings, the credulous nature of its people and other associations must have made him choose his particular form and style for expounding the truths that were torturing him for a long time. The Shaikh had kept them secret for a sufficiently long time, and it was at Makkah that he felt the urgent need of expression. He writes that If he had not written the *Futuhat,* he would have been set on fire. He was absolutely right in saying so. Truth cannot be hidden for a long time. Midas' wife required a hole to bawl out "Midas has ears of an ass." And the Great Shaikh of Andalusia sought relief through the *Futuhat.*

On his arrival at Makkah he began friendship with a scholarly lady and wrote poems extolling her beauty and scholarship. When taken to task for this crime, he wrote an elaborate commentary on his poems giving the whole work a mystic turn to escape the charge that he had sung of carnal love.

This is not the solitary occasion when he gave such a turning to his words. It was his custom to re-sing his poetry giving a completely new meaning. Once he sang as follows.

"Ya man yarani wa la arahu

Kam dha arahu wa la yarani."

(O Thou who seest me, while I see not Thee,

How oft I see Him, while He sees not me!)

When rebuked by his friends, he resang it as follows:

"Ya man yarani mujriman

Wa la arahu akhidha.

Kam dha arahu mun'iman

Wa la yarani la'idha."

(O Thou who seest me *ever prone to sin* Whilst Thee I see not *willing to upbraid* How oft I see Him *grant His grace's aid* Whilst me He sees not *seeking grace to win.)*

He was a *Zahiri* (Conformist) in religion like Ibn Hazm and others. He professed to hold exactly the same religion as the orthodox and was a *batini* (esotericist) in his inner beliefs. His sole guide was the inner light with which he believed himself illuminated in a special way. The different religions were in his opinion equivalent.

The Great Shaikh said: "It was reported to me at Makkah that a woman from Baghdad was praising me very much. I was glad and coferred on her the merits of my circumambulating during the whole of the month of Rajab. After a time a stranger came to me and said: 'While I was sleeping in my garden, I saw thousands of camels laden with musk, ambergris and pearls. I wondered at the magnitude of the wealth and enquired whose it was. I was told that the wealth belonged to Ibne 'Arabi who had presented it to such and such a woman.' He gave the name of the woman also. I had never informed anyone of my dedication. Then I sent for the woman and demanded presents from her in return. She said: 'Once I was sitting in front of the House (the Ka'ba) and you were going round it. I liked you immensely, and the people around me praised you very much. Then I dedicated the merits of my Monday and Thursday doings to you. On both these days I fasted and gave alms.' (The Shaikh writes) I knew that what I gave her was but a fraction of what she had given unto me, for she preceded in her generosity."

Ibne 'Arabi, as already pointed out, was or pretended to be a believer in dreams. In his works there is a collection of dreams in which he saw prophet Muhammad (PBUH) and held converse with him and reports of dreams in which others saw Muhammad (PBUH).

In speaking of the dreams of Ibne 'Arabi, it would be absolutely unfair to paint him as a dreamer. He speaks of visions, sights and the world of *mithal* or ideas. His visions have an inner significance and certain bare truths and ideas are expressed in that peculiar form. The reader should bear in mind that the visions of Ibne 'Arabi are not dreams but a perception into the inner realities of things as perceived by him. His belief in dreams proper was confined to their efficacy in helping individuals, by constant practice, and applications to attain clairvoyance. Unless the above fact is borne in mind a reader is likely to mistake the Great Shaikh, a pillar of rationalism and free thought, to be a credulous dreamer and dupe of visions and illusions.

The Shaikh writes in the introduction to the *Futuhat*: "As I was writing this introduction, I saw through illumination Muhammad (PBUH) in the world of real ideas near the Great Presence. When I saw him there as the chief, he welcomed me and said: 'Here is a quality common to both of us !' Then a pulpit was ordered for in that awful place. On tbe top of the pulpit was written: 'This is the sacred place of Muhammad, he who mounted it inherited the custody of truths and realities and became the guardian of the Church *(Shari'at)*.' At that place I was given all wisdom and endowed with concise speaking. I thanked Allah and mounted the pulpit till I reached the place of Muhammad. Several pieces of white cloth were placed on the place touched by Muhammad's feet, so that my feet might not touch that sacred place." Then the Shaikh gives a long conversation between him and the Holy Prophet.

Once, while circumambulating the Ka'bah, he met a celestial spirit in the form of a youth engaged in the same holy rite, who showed him the living esoteric temple which is concealed under the lifeless exterior, just as the eternal substance of Divine ideas is hidden by the veils of popular religion. These veils the lofty mind must penetrate to reach the splendour within and partake of the Divine character and behold what no mortal eye can endure to look upon.

Ibne 'Arabi swooned at once. When he recovered, he was directed to contemplate the visionary form and to write down the mysteries that it might unveil to his gaze. Then the youth entered the Ka'bah with Ibne 'Arabi and resuming his spiritual aspect appeared to him on a three-legged steed. The youth then breathed into the breast of Ibne 'Arabi the knowledge of all things and once more bade him describe the heavenly form in which all mysteries are enshrined.

Such is the reputed origin of the "Makkan Inspirations" of which the greater portion was written in that town itself. The author claims that every word of them was dictated to him by supernatural means. It may be highly astonishing to a student of Ibne 'Arabi that a profound scholar and rationalist like him should claim knowledge through supernatural means, knowledge of all things, etc.

In this connection the following saying of the Great Shaikh should be borne in mind: "It is not improper on the part of a teacher to tell his pupils that he knows everything and that the knowledge that he can impart cannot be had anywhere else. For this inspires confidence in the teacher and helps the student to acquire knowledge quickly."

Although Ibne 'Arabi performed the pilgrimage of Hajj, in a marvellous passage he has given quite an independent interpretation of the whole ceremony. He says: "Hajj is incumbent on those that consider it to be so. Ihram keeps you off sins temporarily, cultivate the habit of regarding yourself as if you are in Ihram throughout your life. Abstinence is the real significance of fasting and prayers. I am mad after the anklets and rings of my beloved. So I go round the Ka'bah in circles. When I throw stones, I strike at my inner Satan who allures and coys me. When I offer sacrifice at Mina, I slaughter my evil thoughts." Even this passage ends with a description of the honeyed cheeks of his beloved, the fragrance emanating from her person, etc.

In interpreting Ibne 'Arabi's love-poem the following saying of his in *Fusus al-Hikam* must be borne in mind. "Allah is never seen immaterially, and the vision of him in woman is the most perfect of all (page 245).

One of the most elegant poems of Ibne 'Arabi has been beautifully rendered into English by E.G. Browne. The original poem occurs in *Nafh ut-Tib,* the best biography of Ibne 'Arabi available at present. The following is the English translation:

"My soul is much concerned with Her,
Although Her face I cannot see;
Could I behold Her face indeed,
Slain by Her blackened brows I'd be;
And when my sight upon Her fell,
I fell a captive to my Sight,
And passed the night bewitched by Her
And still did rave when dawn grew bright.
Alas ! for my resolves so high!
Did high resolve avail, I say,

The beauty of that Charmer shy,
Would not have made me thus to stray
In beauty as a tender fawn,
Whose pasture the Wild Assessken;
Whose coy regard and half-turned head
Make captives of the souls of Men !
Her breath so sweet as it would seem
As fragrant musk does yield delight.
She's radiant as the midday Sun,
She's as the Moon's Effulgence bright.
If She appear, Her doth reveal
The splendour of the Morning fair;
If She Her tresses loose, the Moon
Is hidden by Her night-black hair.
Take Thou my heart, but leave, I pray
O Moon, athwart the darkest Night,
Mine Eyes, that I may gaze on Thee,
For all my joy is in my sight"

CHAPTER IV

AT DAMASCUS

The Shaikh left Makkah at the end of the year 611 A.H. (1214-15 A.C.) and reached Aleppo in the following year. The Christian Governor of Asia Minor received him with great honour and gave him a large house to live in. While he was thus living in Asia Minor, he visited all important cities of the land and enrolled disciples and admirers everywhere. His fame and talents were at their zenith and princes vied with one another in honouring him.

The Shaikh himself was quite indifferent to wealth and gave out whatever he got in the way of the Lord. He was not against wealth. He called it one of the means of endearing one's self to Allah. But personally he preferred to give his all in charity.

One day, when the Shaikh was living in the big house presented by the Governor of Asia Minor, a beggar approached him and asked him if he could give anything in the way of Allah. The Shaikh said that he has nothing to give except the house in which he was living and offered the house to the beggar. The beggar accepted the offer and the Shaikh vacated the house immediately.

By such acts of extreme generosity and supreme liberality which he had inherited from his famous ancestor, Hatim al-Ta'i, the Shaikh endeared himself to the high and the low, and even his deadliest enemies were not bold enough to violate his personal dignity and lay hands on his holy person, His extreme piety, asceticism, immense knowledge and awe-inspiring personality kept his enemies at arm's length, and all venerated him and hailed him as a living saint of Allah.

The Great Shaikh wandered from city to city in search of a suitable place for settling down once for all, and he decided to live at Damascus. The Chief Qadi of that city, Shamsuddin Ahmed al Khuwa'i, served him like a slave. His works were freely transcribed and circulated. There was no strong opposition in the city. Even if there were any opponents, they were absolutely powerless. The Chief Qadi of the Malikites gave him his daughter in marriage,

After settling at Damascus, the Shaikh had an easy time. He was much revered and amply paid. The Governor of Hems sent him 100 *dirhams* a day and Ibn al-Azki 30 *dirhams*. He took whatever was necessary for his expenses and bestowed all the rest on the poor and the needy.

He confined himself to teaching and writing his voluminous works. He was a great writer and it is said that during the time he was writing the *Futuhat*, he used to write at the rate of three Kararis (about three quires) a day.

The Shaikh developed marvellous psyohic powers and was a great spiritualist. Fantastic powers of dragging in the souls of prophets, attending the Presence of Allah, even summoning Him to be present and making all of them materialise are attributed to him by his favourite disciple Sadruddin of Qonia.

A man in Damascus imprecated Ibne 'Arabi ten times a day as a duty. He died and the Shaikh attended his funeral. Returning home, Ibne 'Arabi sat down facing the Ka'bah. Breakfast was served to him but he did not heed it. He continued like this till after supper time. Then suddenly he turned round happily and demanded his supper which he ate very heartily. He was asked about it, and he said: "I declared to Allah that I would neither eat nor drink till the man who was imprecating me was pardoned. I recited *La ilaha illallah* seventy thousand times till Allah pardoned him."

A son was born to the Shaikh at Malta in the month of Ramdan, 618 A.H. The son studied *Hadith* and was teaching others. He was a good poet and left a Diwan behind him which is very popular.

The Great Saint passed away at the zenith of his glory, much loved and honoured throughout the Islamic world. He lived for seventy eight years, seven months and nine days according to the lunar computation and died on the night preceding Friday, the 28th of Rabl' ul-Akhir, 683 A.H. (1240 A.C.) and was buried below Mount Qasiyun now called Salah which is considered to be a part of paradise. Yafa'i narrates that the Shaikh was teaching his works to one of his pupils when he breathed his last.

Thus died the greatest of the Sufis, seer of the realities of existence, poet of rare talent, scholar of high merit, eminent saint of his age and master of men's hearts and brains. He well merited the title of Shaikh al-Akbar, the Greatest Shaikh, and was also called Hujjatullahil Zahira (the outward proof of Allah) and A'yatullahil Bahira (the astounding miracle of Allah).

His son died in Damascus in 659 A.H., the year when Hulaku entered Baghdad and killed the Khalif Musta'sim. He was buried near his great father in Mount Qasiyun.

CHAPTER V

HIS WORKS

The Shaikh was a great writer and wrote a very large number of volumes. He himself drew up an inventory in 1234 A.C., about five years before his death, enumerating 289 of his writings. Jami in his *Nafhat ul-Uns* credits to him five hundred books. It certainly cannot be. When the Shaikh wrote the inventory he was about 73 years of age and at that advanced age he could not have written many books within a short period of about five years. He wrote a commentary of the first half of the Quran for general readers in fifteen volumes. His work reached the verse *Wama 'allamna hu min al dumna 'Ilma* of surah Kahaf. As he died, he could not finish it. This work, in the words of Majduddin, "is a great book. Each journey is like that on a boundless sea". Another commentary of the Quran in eight volumes for Sufis is also attributed to Ibne 'Arabi.

In short, Ibne 'Arabi was a writer of "great fecundity" and may be considered as one of the most voluminous writers of Islam. The rate of production and his marvellous intellect and imagination are especially to be wondered at when we consider the highly abstruse nature of his works. At a moderate estimate, the number of his works can be reckoned at about three hundred, and of them one hundred and fifty have been catalogued by Brockelmann as existing at present in the various libraries of the East and the West.

Of the writings of all ancient scholars, whose works are available in such a large measure, the exact nature of Ibne 'Arabi's writings is the least known to the modern world. Till now, as far as my knowledge goes, and eminent scholars like R. A. Nicholson and E. G. Browne have also declared, no systematic study of Ibne 'Arabi's works has been attempted.

Even for veteran scholars, it is not possible to understand the Shaikh easily. To understand him one has to get one self saturated with all Islamic sciences including Islamic and pre-Islamic mythology and get an insight into the workings of Muslim scholars. Even for such a scholar, it would be a life-work to analyse the Shaikh's principal works and evolve a consistent philosophy which could be safely called the philosophy of Ibne 'Arabi.

1. *Al-Futuhat al-Makkiyya* is the chief work of Ibne 'Arabi. The author claims that every word of it was inspired by supernatural sources and it contains nothing but truths and realities. The mysterious way in which the great book was commenced has been described in detail in the chapter dealing with the Shaikh's stay at Makkah. The book is now available in four big volumes and was first printed at Bulak in Egypt, in the year 1274 A.C., thirty four years after his death. Till then several copies of it were made, and people considered it to be an act of great merit and means of obtaining the Great Shaikh's blessings to copy this wonderful work.

   'Abd al-Wahhab al Sha'rani has epitomised the book and the epitome is called *Al-Yawaqltu wal Jawahir.* He has also written a strong defence of the book and its author; The *Futuhat* itself contains 560 chapters of which chapter 559 contains a summary of the whole and is a masterly treatise expounding the views of Ibne 'Arabi on all matters of religion and faith in a way peculiar to himself. The question of Allah and His nature is discussed in several parts of the book under different heads. The opening lines contain a concise exposition of the question in the usual clever way of the author. There are chapters dealing with the soul, its nature, origin, etc. The question of prophethood and inspiration has been tackled in detail. The whole question of predestination, Day of Judgment, punishment and reward, hell and heaven, has been discussed. The related topics of the Quran, the Throne of Allah, the Great Table, the Pen and the creation of Adam have all been dealt with in their entirety. Besides, all the principles of jurisprudence, law and theology have been discussed in the most wonderful manner.

The style and method of treatment of the book are uncommon. It was not possible for the author in the interest of his life and the preservation of his book to write in direct language. A most abstruse and fantastic style was chosen so that it might not be possibte for the credulous theologians to understand it.

2. Next to *Al-Futuhat al-Makkiyya,* comes *Fusus al-Hikam,* begun in Damascus in the beginning of 627 A.H. It was fitho-graphed with the commentary of Abdur Razzaq al-Kashani at Cairo in 1309 A.C.

The *Fusus* is a short work in twenty seven chapters, each of which is named after one of the prophets. It is highly esteemed and has been the subject of numerous commentaries in Arabic, Persian and Turkish. This book and *Al-Futuhat al-Makkiyya* form the two principal works of the author. R. A. Nicholson has made a study of the *Fusus* and published notes on it in his book. *Studies in Islamic Mysticism.* Khaja Khan has made a synoptical translation of this work into English under the title, *Wisdom of the Prophets.*

The style and form of the *Fusus* are also very abstruse and it requires much patience to make a thorough study of it.

The title of the book literally means "Bezels of Wisdom" or "Mosaic of Precepts". This book was.completed in the 3 years 1230 A.C. at Damascus. It is said that this work also, like its bigger comrade, was undertaken after the Prophet Muhammad appeared to the author.

3. *Mashahidul Asrar* and

4. *Matali' al-Anwar-al-Ilahiyyah* were written at Qonia in 1209 A.C.

5. *Insha al-Dawaīr* is devoted to the explanation of man's place in creation and cosmogony.

6. *Uqlat al-Mustawfid* describes the denizens of the upper world and of this lower one, the spirits,

the Throne of Allah, the stars, the earth, etc., in his own mystical way.

7. *Tuhafat al-Safara* details the stages of the mystic's journey towards the knowledge of Allah.

8. *Hilyat al-Abdal* (Ornament of the Ascetics), a guide to happiness, was written at Ta'if near Makkah in 1202 A.C.

9. *Kimiya al-Sa'adah* treats of the properties and virtues of the formula of the belief in one Allah.

10. *Ifada* (Information) speaks of the three fundamental branches of knowledge—Allah, the rational world and the world of sense.

11. A certain number of his treatises deal with the occult sciences as his *Studies of the Jafr*, a Cabalistic work ascribed to 'Ali bin Abi Talib.

12. *Faida* (Utility) turns on the subject of divination by means of the letters of the alphabet.

I was not fortunate enough even to see any of the works numbered 3 to 12. I got the information given above from Clement Huart's book, *A History of Arabic Literature*. I hope the subjects of the above books are as stated by the learned scholar. Though these works may profess to deal with topics like "the denizens of the upper world," "the Throne of Allah," etc, from an intimate knowledge of the Shaikh's principal works, I am bold enough to conjecture that these works contain invaluable pearls covered in unwholesome shells.

13. *Tarjuman al-Ashwaq* is a collection of Sufi poetry published at Makkah in 1201 A.C. He wrote a commentary on this work and gave all the poems a mystic turn. These poems have been collected and translated into English by R.A. Nicholson.

14. *Muhadarat al-Abrar* deals with literary and historical topics.

15. The Commentary, sufficient notice of which has already been taken. His other noteworthy works are:

16. *Kitabul Akhlaq.*

17. *Amr Muhakkam.*

18. *Majmi' al-Rasail al-Ilahiyyah.*

19. *Mawaqi' al-Nujum* written at Maria when he visited that place in 595 A.H.

Besides some of the works mentioned above, *Al-Maqqari* gives the following names of his works as important.

20. *Al-Jam'u wa al-Tafsil fi Haqaiq al-Tanzil.*

21. *Al-Jadhwat al-Muqtabisat.*

22. *Al-Ma'arif al-Ilahiyyah.*

23. *Al-Asra'ila Maqam il Asria.*

24. *'Anqa al-Mu'ghrib.*

25. *Fadail 'Abdil Aziz al-Mahduwl.* The works of Ibne 'Arabi are too many to be mentioned. As I have already said it is not easy to find out even the nature of these works. They cannot be easily analysed. The brief description given above must be impressions gathered from a cursory glance into some of these works.

Of the above-mentioned twenty-five works only Nos. 1, 2,3, 7, 13, 15, 18, 19 and 20 have been printed till now. The other available works not yet printed are found scattered in different libraries of the world. Many more of the missing works of Ibne 'Arabi may be recovered in a few years. The library movement in the East is not strong enough, so hundreds of valuable manuscripts are rotting in the most unsuited quarters.

CHAPTER IV

THE SAYINGS OF IBNE 'ARABI

1. The speech of a knower must be in accordance with the understanding of the hearer, his weakness and permanent hidden prejudices.

2. If you find it difficult to answer anyone, do not answer him. His vessel is full and he does not require an answer.

3. An ass knows more than one who knows only something about the unity of Allah.

4. Flee from suspicions.

5. Many people give directly opposite interpretations to sayings of scholars.

6. If a knower gives out what passes in his mind, the veterans consider him to be ignorant; the orthodox retort and shun him. The truth is, Allah has given His beloved, miracles which are but a kind of the miracles of Prophets. It is not improper

to talk in their own way because some scholars are not able to understand them.

7. If one does not believe in what a group says, he must not keep their company; for company without understanding is a fatal poison.

8. Close proximity is a veil just like great distance is one. If Allah is nearer to us than the jugular vein, where are the seventy thousand veils ?

9. Do not admit doubt in knowledge of Divine secrets, for its proper place is in the exact sciences.

10. The qualification of a perfect man in his generosity towards his enemies who do not know the nature and character of Allah and call themselves his enemies on account of their ignorance although he (the perfect man) is always generous towards them.

11. The qualification of a Shaikh is that he should possess all that the *murid* (disciple) may require of him, not miracles and illumination.

12. The Sufi is one who drops away the three "i's." He shall not say li (for me), nor '*indi* (with me) nor *mata'i* (my wealth). This is, he must not attribute anything to himself.

13. Supplication is the marrow of worship. It is through the marrow that the limbs are strong. Similarly, it is by supplication that the devotion of a worshipper is strengthened.

14. A man cannot attain the stage of perfect knowledge, if he ignores a single injunction of any of the prophets' religion. He who claims this stage and transgresses any of the injunctions of the Islamic faith is a liar.

15. Complete ignorance of Allah is sure knowledge of Allah.

16. The names of Allah on which the existence of the universes is based are but four, the Living, the Mighty, the Seeker and the Knower, and it is through these four names that His being a Allah is proved.

17. He who deviates from the Code, never attains anything, though his fame may reach the heavens.

18. Allah, the merciful, has prohibited the blind following of Malik, Ahmed, No'man or others.

19. I am not a man who says Ibn Hazm said so and so, Ahmeḍ said so and so and No'man said so and so.

20. O Pearl Divine, white Pearl that in a shell.

Of dark mortality are made to dwell !
Alas, while common gems we prize and hoard.
Thy worth inestimable is still ignored!

CHAPTER VII

OPINIONS OF SCHOLARS ABOUT THE SHAIKH

Scholars are definitely divided in their opinions about Shaikh al-Akbar. One group led by Ibn al-Taimia, al-Taftazani and Ibrahim al Biqa'i denounces him as an infidel and charges him with the advocacy of Hului (incarnation) and Ithihat (monism), while another group headed by Majduddin, the author of *Al-Qamus,* Suyuti and 'Abdur Razzaq al Kashani defends him strongly and considers him to be a great saint. Sufi of a high order, *Siddiq* and defender for the faith.

The Shaikh himself never cared for what his opponents said. He never stooped down to write replies to their attacks but went on with his work calmly and coolly. Yet it will be great interest and value to record the opinions of these scholars for the information of the reader.

Unfortunately, the exact remarks of the Shaikh's opponents and extracts from their works are not available to me at Madras. Nor have I been able to gather any detailed information about them from writers of the East or the West. The nature of the charges levelled against the Shaikh is to be found only in the writings of his defenders.

'Allamah Jamaluddin writes of him: "I saw Muhiyuddin at Damascus. He was the greatest of the scholars of the path. He combined in him all the acquirable arts and those arts and qualities that are conferred by Allah. He occupied a very prominent place and he has written many works. He was obsessed with the idea of unity through study and Nature, even when he was in a trance. He had scholars and people falling into transports as his followers. Among his followers there were many authors also. Between him and my teacher, Al-Harrar, there was brotherliness and affection."

Ibn Kamal Basha says in his *Fatwa:* "Know ye all men that Ibne 'Arabi al-Ta'i al-Andalusi is a perfect *Mujtahid* with rare accomplishments and strange miracles. He who opposes him does wrong, and he who persists in condemning him goes astray; and it is incumbent on the Sultan to punish such one."

Munawi says that men were divided in their opinions of Ibne 'Arabi. Some called him *Zindiq* and some others *Siddiq* and chief of the saints. Some scholars went to the extent of prohibiting the reading of his books. This fact is corroborated by Shaikh Burhanuddin in his *Mu'jam*.

Jalaluddin Suyuti has written a book in defence of Ibne 'Arabi called *Tanbihl Ghabi bi Tanziati Ibn il'Arabi*.

Shaikh al Nawa also writes that the opinion of scholars about Ibne 'Arabi varied from infidelity to saintship.

Ibn Hajr writes that some called him a *Siddiq* and others an apostle of Satan.

Ibn al-Maqri writes in his book *Rouda* "Doubting the infidelity of the Ibne 'Arabi group is infidelity."

'Abd al Wahhab al Sha'rani, the great scholar who has made an epitome of the great *Al-Futuhat al-Makkiyya,* considers Ibne 'Arabi to be a great saint.

The saint Najmuddin Isbahani and Taj bin Ataullah of Alexandria have praised him as a great scholar and profound Sufi.

It was asked of Majduddin Ferozadi, the author of *Al-Qamus,* whether it was advisable to read the works of Ibne 'Arabi. In reply to the question the famous Qadi wrote a book named *Al-Ightibatu bi Mu'alajati Ibn il-Khayyat*. In it he writes:

"The Great Shaikh was a Shaikh of the Path, knowledge and exposition and *Imam* of research in matters real and ceremonial. As for his books and contemplations they are surging oceans whose pearls and extent are unknown. Allah's knowledge is confined only to such people as deserve it. The peculiarity of his books is that if one reads them and contemplates, his heart will be widened, his difficulties met and knotty problems solved. This is not possible except by those on whom the choicest blessings of Allah pour down and his special sources of knowledge are opened. He has written four hundred books and left a commentary on the Quran incomplete. He was a man of *wilayat* (saintship) and *siddiqiyyah* (evertruth fulness). Some try to ignore him and the ignorant go to the extent, of calling him an infidel. It is due to nothing but a lack of understanding of the import of his sayings and actions and poetry. Their unfortunate hands have not reached the fruits on account of their shortness."

Shaikh al-Islam Salahuddin and a host of other reliable Shaikhs report of the servant of 'Izzuddin Ibn 'Abd al-Salam as follows: "Once, we were in the classroom of Shaikh 'Izzuddin Ibn 'Abd al-Salam. A discussion on the root of the word *Zindiq* ensued. One enquired whether it was Arabic or Persian in origin. One of the scholars said that it was an Arabicised Persian word and that its origin was *Zan din* (woman's creed), *i.e.*, hiding infidelity and professing faith. Another asked: 'Like whom ?' A man on the side of 'Izzuddin Ibn 'Abd al-Salam remarked: 'Like Ibne 'Arabi in Damascus."' The Shaikh did not talk; nor did he oppose the statement. It so chanced that on that day I fasted and the Shaikh invited me to breakfast with him. He was highly courteous and kind to me. I asked him: 'Sir, do you know the most eminent saint of our age?' He said: 'What is that to you; eat on.' I found out that he knew the thing. I stopped eating and pressed him in the name of Allah to let me know the person. He smiled and said: 'Shaikh Muhiyuddin Ibne 'Arabi.' I remained silent and astonished for a time. The Shaikh asked what as the cause of my wonder. I said I wondered beca that very morning a man had branded him as a *Zindiq* and he had kep quiet and now he stated that Muhiyuddin was the Kutub of the age. He said: "Keep quiet, it was an assembly of jurists'."

Shaikh Kamaluddin al-Zamlaqani, one of the great Shaikhs of Syria, writes: "How ignorant are those people that oppose the Shaikh Muhiyuddin Ibne 'Arabi! His great sayings and precious words which occur in his writings are too great for their understanding. Let them bring them to me for explanation of difficult passages, I shall show them their import, so that they may know the truth and give up misunderstanding. He wrote the *Fusus* under instructions from the Prophet and he was asked to go among men and spread knowledge."

Dhahabi writes: "I do not at all doubt that Muhiyuddin is deliberately telling lies wholly. He is among the chief heretics and a hardened Sufi."

R. A. Nicholson calls the writings of Ibne 'Arabi "abstruse, fantastic and interminable speculations "which Ibne 'Arabi presents to his readers in the guise of Heavenly Truths," and says that "it will not be easy to sketch even the outlines of his Theosophical system until the copious materials at our disposal have been more thoroughly studied by some European scholar interested in Sufism." Further, he says that "Ibne 'Arabi combined in him the most extravagant mysticism with the straightest orthodoxy." About the views of the Shaikh, he writes: "Ibne Arabi appears to have set his face against the extreme pantheistic tendencies which characterised Persian Sufism. With all his marvellous visions and inspirations, his prophetic vision and luxuriant fancy which delighted in Pythagorean theories of numbers and letters, he did not allow himself to forget that the Divine and human natures are essentially different. Even Muhammad (PBUH), as he points out, remained at two bows length's distance from Allah. True union is one of will and not of essence."

The following is the opinion of L. Massignon, Professeur au College *do* France, Paris, about Ibne 'Arabi expressed in a letter to Khaja Khan published along with Khaja Khan's book *Wisdom of the Prophets*: "As you know it already, my impression is and remains that Mansur Hallaj by one single supernatural rush dived deeper through the waves of mystical love towards the Real—while Ibn 'Arabi, with all his elaborated differentiations and emanations, does not bear such a pathetic witness before the seeker, of Allah's transcendential abode and supreme personality. I should accordingly value some of the former's short and burning utterances in his *Tawasin* and elsewhere over several of the latter's more logically planned sentences."

D.B. MacDonald describes the Shaikh's works as "a strange jumble of Theosophy and metaphysical paradoxes, all much like the Theosophy of our day."

I have given in brief the opinions of scholars, both ancient and modern, about the Great Shaikh and his works. Opinions vary immensely. It is true that many have not understood the real significance of the Shaikh's writings. For a thorough examination of the question, whether the Shaikh was really orthodox or not, no through knowledge of his works is required. It can be easily asserted after going through a few books of his that the views of the Shaikh were not in accordance with the common faith of the man in the street.

The theologians were quite right in denouncing him as a heretic; for any casual observer, especially a modern observer, can very easily find out what he was. But to determine whether he was a monist or not requires a complete study of his works with this question in view.

In the following pages I give a short account of the Great Shaikh's views on certain important topics such as Allah, prophethood and inspiration. Since many of the questions are very delicate, I have given as far as possible the literal translations of the Shaikh's own passages to avoid commitments except to thy extent of accurate translation. Often, I had to mutilate passages for the sake of brevity.

CHAPTER VIII

ON ALLAH
Unity of Existence

Allah created all things from nothing and His own nothingness, and made His Word the cause of their existence, so that we may find out the secret of their beginning or beginninglessness from His beginninglessness.

His power manifested itself. It became manifest and manifested, it never declined. But He remained in hiding and hidden. He is called the First and the Last, the Apparent and the Hidden. This diversity is in the stages *(manazil)* and is evident in the media of manifestation of the stages. Abd al-Halim is not Abd al-Karim, and Abd al-Ghafur is not Abd al-Shakur. For every man there is a name of which he is the master. He is the body and that name is the mind.

If a person calls Allah, He is the Addresser and the Addressed. If a creature does what he is ordered to do, He is the Obeyed and the Obeyer. When this truth bewildered me, I sang in my usual way:

The Lord's Real, the Creature's Real;
I long to know who does dictate:
If "Man", say ye, he does perish
If "Allah", say ye, I do dictate.
(Al-Futuhat al 'Makkiyya, Vol. 1, p.2)

When Allah wanted to see the forms of His names, that is, to see His own form in a Creation attributed with His own names, He exhibited His full grandeur. He exhibited His own secret to Himself; i.e., He saw it in a creature that exhibited all His attributes so that His own secret manifested itself to Him. He was observant of His own Self before manifestation; but this observance was not the same as observance of self in another. In the former case, there is no necessity for an external figure; while in the latter there is. When He wanted to see His essence through His attributes, He made the form of the Cosmos in the shape of a symmetrical figure.

All the names of Allah became manifest in man; and hence, man controls everything in the world. Allah reprimanded the angels about this very man; they were not aware of his worth; for everybody could know only so much of Allah as his capacity allowed him.

Thus Allah explained Himself in terms of our attributes. When we observe our attributes, we observe the attributes of Allah. He is without beginning and without end. He is the First with reference to us, and He is the Last similarly. We emerged out of Him, He is the First; we merge unto Him, He is the Last.

(Al-Fasl Adamiyyah)

Perception of Allah is of two kinds— either of the person or of the names. The perception of the person is an illumination of Allah, and this illumination will be in the form, of which the illuminated has the capacity, and not in any other. Hence the illuminated sees his own form in the mirror of Allah and does not see Allah. If you look into a mirror, the mirror disappears and you see your own form. This is the highest stage, to which a creature can reach. Do not aspire to anything higher and get puzzled. Allah is not in the higher regions. There is nothing beyond except complete nothingness. In enabling you to see yourself, He becomes your mirror; and in manifesting His names you become His mirror.

His names or aspects are more innumerable than the sands on the seashore. Names are only relationships of the essence with particular attributes, which are only aspects of the essence. One name is differentiated from another name in manifestation; while in its internal nature, it is the same as that another.

"He who understands his self understands Allah." Gnosis gives him a glimpse of a manifestation of Allah, which is his beatific vision and which he gets even in this world, and more clearly in the next. If he does not get it here, he will not have it in the hereafter. "Whoever is blind here, shall also be blind in the hereafter and more erring from the way." *(Al-Fasl Shethiyya)*

Mystics see that Allah is One and All and One in All.

Sublimity belongs to Allah alone. The essences of things are in themselves non-existent deriving what existence they possess from Allah, who is the real substance of all that exists.

The One brought number into being and the number analysed the One. He that knows this, knows that the Creator who is declared to be incomparable is the creatures which are compared with Him by reason of His manifesting Himself in their forms— albeit the creatures have been distinguished from the Creator. The Creator is the creature and the creature is the Creator. All this proceeds from one essence and the many individualised essences. The world of Nature is many forms in one mirror; nay, one Form in diverse mirrors.

Bewilderment arises from the difference of views; but those who perceive the truth of what I have stated are not bewildered.

The Sufi considers that worship means knowledge which is the means of securing sight.

(Al-Fasl Shethiyya)

Noah did not call his people to unity in diversity, and to diversity in the midst of unity. If he had of alled them to both aspects they would have accepted him.

(Al-Fasl Nuhiyyah)

One of Allah's beautiful names is 'All (the Elevated). Since there is no stranger *(ghair)* in the Universe, to what can he be superior ? He is the essence of things, hence things are by themselves elevated. The reality is: all is One in totality; multipli-city is in aspects; and aspects are relationships which do not exist. The reality is one in existence which is the essence: it is, therefore, elevated in itself. We, therefore, say that each manifestation is Himself. Abu Sa'yd al-Khurraz, who is one of the tongues of Allah, says: "Allah cannot be recognised unless He manifests Himself in contraries; and in spite of the contraries you must recognise His Oneness. He is the First; He is the Last. He is the Apparent; He is the Hidden. In existence He sees Himself, and there is none else to see Him, and there is none else from whom He can be hidden His names are Abu Sa'yd al-Khurraz and others."

The reality of all is the same, although the directions or sides are different; for when the number revolves several times, it becomes many: in fact one is the originator of many, e.g., 9 in the descending scale and 10 in the ascending, up to infinity, are one. The reality of all figures has a special rank, but is the totality of the same "ones."

Thus Allah unmanifest is the same as Allah manifest, although the two are differentiated. The Creator is the created and the created is the Creator. The same reality is one and many. The same essence is the many essences.

(Al-Fasl Idrisiyyah)

Do you not see that Allah manifests Himself in the attributes of transient things, and in the attributes of defection and decay pertaining to them ? Do you not know that the created appears with the attributes of Allah?

How is Allah entirely idependent, when I help Him and make Him good ?

'Ayn or reality is the aptitudes of Allah and was not created by him. The aptitudes or the "Known" in the knowledge of Allah appear in the mirror of Self and the Self manifests Itself according to them.

When one thing permeates another, the one becomes hidden in the other. If the Creator is manifest, the created is hidden, then all the names of Allah like Seer and Hearer become the names of the created. If the created is manifest, then Allah is hidden in it, and the sight and hearing of the created become Allah's right and hearing.

The Divine essence, which is all that exists, may be regarded from two aspects: *(a)* as a pure simple attributeless essence: *(b)* as an essence endowed with attributes. Allah, considerd absolutely, is beyond relation and therefore beyond knowledge—inconceivable and ineffable. From this point of view, Allah, in a sense, is not Allah. Some philosophers and Abu Hamid (al-Ghazzali)have asserted that Allah is known without reference to the Universe; but they are mistaken.

(Fusus al-Hikam, p. 74, *Kashani* Edition)

The fate of every individual is his essential character as it exists from eternity in the Divine knowledge.

Men receive of good and evil just what the necessity of their natures demands. The verse, "Had Allah willed, He would have guided you all aright" (The Qur'an, Chapter VI, verse 150), means that Allah could not will the impossible. His wisdom requires that the infinite diversity of His attributes should be matched by infinitely diverse capacities in the objects wherein these attributes are displayed. *(Al-Fasl Ibrahimiyyah)*

Allah says: "Blessed is the person who has the approval of his Lord." There is not anything in the

Universe which has not the approval of its own Lord. For, it alone keeps up the lordship of that Lord, the two things being interrelated and interdependent. Every reality owes its existence to its own Lord, for if the one disappears, the other two will disappear. "You are a secret of *rububiyat* (lordship)," said Suhil at-Tustari.

Thou art man, and thou art Allah;

Whose creature art thou then?

Thou art Allah and thou art man;

Whom dost thou address then ?

(Al-Fasl Ismma'ilahiyyah)

The realities in the knowledge of Allah manifest themselves in a phantasmagoria ever assuming new and varied forms. *(Al-Fasl Ya'kubiyyah)*

The world has no existence of its own, nor is it a mere fancy or thought. It is a fancy in as much as it is not an addition on Allah or extraneous to Him.

Shadow cannot be separated from the person. Thus you know how you are Allah and how you are other than Allah. Allah is both the microcosm and macrocosm—pure and purer. Light appears in the colour which the lantern possesses. It has no colour of its own. The light that appears is the reflection of the glass of the lantern. If a man cleanses his heart, the manifestations of Allah become clearer and more abundantin him. Thus there are amongst us those to whom Allah becomes sight, hearing, etc.; for Allah has said: "I become his hearing and his sight." Such a man comes nearer to Allah than other man.

Thus you and your sensations, which you call other than Allah are mere thought and the world is thought within thought. Existence itself is Allah.

His essence is one and His attributes are many. When the essence is independent of us all, it is named absolute Oneness; and when it manifests its attributes and names, it becomes Oneness in multiplicity. Both these aspects are covered by the title *Ahad* (Single). Our realities are shadows or lights reflected on Himself. As regards existence, He is our reality; and as regards limitations, He is not our reality. *(Al-Fasl Yusufiyyah)*

The Hisness of Allah pervades the organs of the creature. Thus the creature is Allah, and Allah is what is observed in the imaginary world. Allah is what is sensed and the world is what is inferred. Believers and illumi-nated people see Him in this world. For those, who are outside this group, Allah is the inferred and the world is the observed. Allah referred to His own Self as *His ghair or* stranger, and thus pronounced certain actions as forbidden; for all wicked actions are the result of externalities which appear as *ghair.* Allah is the reality of things, and externalities are yourselves. The stranger says that hearing is Zayd's,and the gnostic says that it is Allah's; and so is the case with other faculties. Allah is the reality of the ears, eyes, hands, feet and tọngue, *i.e.*, He is the reality of all bodily and spiritual senses of His creature.

The first; limitation of the Unlimited was the names. The second limitation was the Throne on which He had taken His stand. Then He is said to have descended to the sky and to the earth; and He is said to be the reality of us all. He is the reality of all things. If he were not the reality, nothing would have existed. Everything in the world is His face. He is the Seer and the Seen; He is the Soul of the world.

He who sees Allah in himself with Allah's sight is a gnostic; and he who expects to see Allah with his own eyes on the Day of judgment is an ignoramus (*jahil*). Allah will manifest Himself to His devotee in the form of His belief. But you do not confine Him to any particular form; He is above limitations; so you must become a believer in all forms of beliefs. "Wherever thou turnest thy face, there is the face of the Lord." The face refers to the *dhat* or essence of Allah which is His reality and which is everywhere and in everything So, Allah has warned gnostics not to become oblivious to the observance of this reality in this short span of life, for man is not aware when he will breathe his last. One who dies in this observation is quite different from one who dies without it. Allah's own servants, however, turn their faces towards the sacred House of Makkah in their prayers, for they believe when praying that there is Allah there. This also is an aspect of Allah's aspects. You do not confine Him there, you simply show respect to that direction in your discernment. *(Al-Fasl Hudiyyah)*

The Divine essence is knowing in itself, knows all things in itself and distinguishes them from itself as objects of its knowledge. The difference, of course, does not impair the essential unity of knowledge, knower and known. Human actions are logically self-determined. *(Fusus al-Hlkam,* p. 77)

An eternal essence is known, but it is not known to be Allah, *i.e.*, an object of worship. While Allah is independent of created beings in respect of His essence, He requires them in respect of His Divinity.
(Ma'budiyat, Fusus al-Hikam, p. 78)

Allah's knowledge of essence is His knowledge of all individual souls. The soul, as a mode of Divine being, determines its own destiny. Every one's portion in this world is that which Allah knows he will receive and which is all that he is capable of reciving, Allah Himself can, ofcourse, alter it any time.

Sin is disobedience to law: it cannot be disobedience to Divine will. Reward and punishment in the future life may be regarded as effects of obedience or disobedience, *i.e.*, Divine manifestations determined by the state of the individual soul, but it is a more profound view that Allah Himself feels the pleasure and the pain.

(*Fusus al-Hikam,* pp. 105-6)

The adept sees unity in diversity; the names are many, their underlying unity is the same. The creature's vision of Allah will be in one of His aspects. The phenomena display one underlying noumenon: all extensions display one essence. "He who understands his self, understands Allah." His self is in the image'of Allah. The creature is the reality of Allah. People do not know this except prophets, saints and great *Sufis.* Con-templation does not extend there. Extension, is always in change. The world is extension, and it is in change every moment "They are in doubt regarding a new creation " The essence is a conglomeration of extensions. Extensions are only the boundaries of the essence. The people of insight see that Allah sends out His manifestations every moment; and these do not repeat themselves. The disappearance of one manifestation is *far.* (annihilation) and the appearance of another is *baqa. Faria* annihilates the world every

moment, and *haqa* rehabilitates it at the every moment.
(Al-Fasl Shu'aibiyyah)

Verily those people became hiders of the truth who said Allah is Jesus, the son of Mary.

It would not have been hiding the truth, if they had said Jesus is Allah, or that Jesus is the son of Mary. They confined Divinity only to the form of Jesus. Some restricted his truth to Mary and referred him to the similitude of Gabriel when he breathed life into birds, and called him the "Word of Allah"; and some others referring to his raising the dead, called him the "Spirit of Allah." These differences have arisen only in the case of Jesus. All created objects are words of Allah which are never annihilated: for they all come under the command *Kun* (be). *(Al-Fasl Isawlyyah)*

Although reality is the same, gradations are necessary in appearance; so much so that we say one man is more knowing than another. Hence do not restrict Him to one appearance, and ignore Him in another while you realise Him in the same. Allah has identified Himself with every hearer and seer amongst the living in this world and the next. All things in the world are instinct with life; but the life of some of them is hidden from the perception of some men: the next world is an abode of life.

Thus, one whose perception of the esoteric aspect of things is more penetrating will have a better perception of Allah than another of ordinary perception; that is, Allah will be more manifest to the one than to the other. Do not, therefore, ignore what I have shown you as variations in the names of Allah. The named is Allah in every case. Thus do not refute those who say that the reality of the created is the reality of Allah.

The world is a dream and it requires an interpretation. *(Al-Fasl Sulaimaniyyah)*

The secret of life or Hisness of Allah permeates water, which is the origin of all elements. "And We created all things out of water." There is nothing in evidence which is not living and there is not a thing existing which does not give out the praise of Allah. We do not understand this expression of praise except through spiritual insight. The Throne of Allah is on water; and water guards it, from below and from within.

Allah created man, and man became proud and desired elevations; and Allah gave him elevation and guards him from beneath and from within. Hence the Prophet said; "If you let down, a bucket by a rope verily it descends to Allah." Thus the relationship of Allah is from below as it is from above also, as in the verses: "They fear Allah from above them", "And He is predominant over His creatures."

Allah said unto Job, Urge with thy foot thy horse, this is a cold bathing place. His body had become heated on account of distress and calamities. Allah gave him rest by cold water. When the creature is in distress, Allah also is in distress, in so far as His Hisness pervades His creation; "And towards Him return all actions": and so far as His *dhat* is concerned He is free and above all these which pertain to the stages of His manifestations.

This world is mystical and transcendental as it is th face of Allah. Allah's existence is manifest from the manifestation of the world, just as man's existence is manifest from the manifestation of his face. Thus in so far as reality is concerned, He is the First; and so far as the face is concerned, he is the Last. So far as changes and states are concerned. He is the Apparent: and so far as the control of these things is concerned, He is the Hidden. "He is cognisant of everything." "-He is witness over all things." Therefore, He is present in and observant of everything. Thus Allah is realised through observation and not through reason and contemplation. *(Al-Fasl Ayyubiyyah)*

When full gnosis dawns upon a man, he possesses it both in qualitylessness and qualitiedness. He realises Allah to be immanent in all forms of elements; and no form remains whose reality is not considered by him to be the reality of Allah. And this realisation gives him perfect gnosis. In the composition of man, imagination dominates over intelligence. Imagination creates a form to which pure intelligence gives a tangible shape. By the aid of imagination, qualitiedness is recognised in qualitylessness; and by the aid of reason qualitylessness is recognised in qualitiedness. The one is not devoid of the other.

Nothing is annihilated in its reality, although its sensible form may be effaced. This immortality of forms is a grace of Allah.

Allah said to Muhammad (PBUH): "Thou didst not throw when thou didst throw but Allah didst throw." To all appearances, it was the Prophet that did throw. Allah threw the sand being in the form of Muhammad (PBUH). Allah was the cause, and He manifested in the form of Muhammad (PBUH) and informed His creatures accordingly. *(Al-Fasl Ilyasiyyah)*

Allah is known by a particular name in a particular aspect: thus one aspect is said to be sky, another earth: the reality is the same in everything as the Ash'ariyyah say, who maintain that essence is the same and extensions are different. The reality appears multitudinous on account of its aspects and their relationships, *e.g.* man is the same as horse in reality or essence; but different from it in its aspect or temperaments.

Do not create a partner with Allah in existence; for *shirk* is a great sin. *Shirk* is division of existence into two. There can be no division. All faces or aspects exhibit one single reality. *Shirk* is the identification of an aspect with reality itself or the identification of one aspect with another. *(Al-Fasl Luqmaniyyah)*

Moses said to Saamari: "What is your answer, Saamari, that you disobeyed Allah and reverted from the absolute Allah to a form and made that image from the ornaments of the people and put the people's heart into it ?"

The true gnostic is one who sees everything worshipped as a manifestation of Allah; hence every worshipped thing gets the name of *ilah* (Allah) besides its own name of stone, tree, animal, man or angel. The latter name is the individualisation of that manifestation Divine, which is a particular manifestation among all the stages of Allah.

Those who said "We do not worship them except that they take us nearer to Allah" (The Quran, XXXIX, 3), did not realise that they worshipped only one out of several and innumerable manifestations. They raised only one manifestation to the rank of Divineness. They said, in the case of the Prophet: "He has converted all Allahs into one Allah. This is a matter for surprise." These people had taken their stand on the multiplicity of forms. The Prophet asked them to give out the names of their Allahs. They gave out the names; and each name had a reality behind it. Gnostics ignore forms in accordance with their faith, although they realise that idolators worship the one Allah in several forms. Allah's know-ledge is *dhouqi* (pertaining to aptitude) and such knowledge is an illumination; and illumination is essential for the manifestation of forms. Thus, one who sees an illumination worships the form in which he sees it, being actuated by his own desire. *(Al-Fasl Haruniyyah)*

The Prophet said: *Kana Allahu wa la shaya ma'hu* "Allah is and nothing is with Him." These words mean that there is only Allah and nothing besides Him. Some think that the verb *kanạ* is used to denote a past state. That is wrong; *kana* here is used for eternity as in *Kana Allahu Ghafuran* (Allah is pardoning). The word denotes past, present and future. So this does not denote a past state, when Allah was alone and none was with Him. Besides, we know that Allah is as He was. So, the meaning of what the Prophet said is that there is Allah alone and nothing besides Him. This clearly means that existence is identical with Him for it is the medium of His manifestation and He is manifested through it. *(Al-Futuhat* Vol. *2,* p. 56)

Allah by Himself makes man obey when He is so pleased and also judges in accordance with the injunctions given to him. It is obligation that has given rise to the term the "worshipped"

"There is no might or strength except through Allah". Allah leads you to good actions and rewards you. So is He designated the "Magnanimous". If Heaven be the reward for what you have done, where is the magnanimity of Allah which is attributed to Him?

You are bestowed the knowledge that you are for yourself. But you are not given the knowledge about the origin of your self. If you are not the author of what you seek recompense for, how do you view your actions?

Cast off the things and their Creator, the sustained and the Sustainer. *(Al-Futuhat,* Vol. I, p. 2)

Allah acquainted Moses that soul does not work up the body except through the body; and so also He does not work up the world except through the world itself, or through the forms of His names. He brings out the offspring through the parent. So also effects depend on causes.

Allah is one, homogeneous in essence and multitudinous in His aspects; just as noumenon is one and displays several phenomena. This display of faces is called *tajalli;* and Allah is manifest in these faces.

Allah spoke to Moses from fire, as Moses was in search of fire. If He had spoken from anything else, Moses would have turned away from Him.

(Al-Fasl Musawiy yah)

Allah has also informed us that He worships us. He becomes a worshipper in His aspect, the Last; for this aspect of Allah' manifests after the existence of the worshipping creature ends. The imagined Allah is what the creature has created for himself. Junayd has said: "The colour of the water is the colour of its vessel." This is a very correct explanation of the above doctrine.

If people understand this doctrine of Junayd, they will accept the Allah of every believer and observe Allah in every form and in all forms. Every one's conception of Allah is according to his own idea and not out of his knowledge.

The believer praises the Allah Who is in the form of his belief and with Whom he has connected himself. He praises none but himself; for his Allah is made by himself and to praise the work is to praise the maker of it; its excellence or imperfection belongs to its maker. For this reason he blames the beliefs of others, which he would not do if he were just.

Beyond doubt, the worshipper of this particular Allah shows ignorance when he criticises others on account of their beliefs. If he understood the saying of Junayd, "the colour of the water is the colour of the vessel containing it," he would not interfere with the beliefs of others, but would perceive Allah in every form and in every belief. He has opinion, not knowledge, therefore Allah said: "I am in My servant's opinion of Me", *i.e.* I do not manifest Myself to him save in the form of his belief. Allah is absolute or restricted as He pleases, and the Allah of religious belief is subject to limitations; for He is the Allah who is contained in the heart of His servant. But the absolute Allah is not contained by anything for He is the being of all things and the being of Himself. And a thing is not said either to contain itself or; not to contain itself.

(Al-Fasl Muhammadiyyah)

The whole infinite series of individuali-sations is in fact one eternal and everlasting manifestation which never repeats itself. *(Fusus,* pp. 153 *et seq* and 239)

Allah is the spirit and the form of the Universe. We must not say that the Universe is but a form of which He is the spirit *(Fusus,* pp. 132 and 146)

All things are attributes of Allah, as such they are ultimately identical with Allah apart from whom they are nothing. *(Fusus,* p. 226)

CHAPTER IX

ON PROPHETHOOD AND MESSENGERSHIP

There are four grades of goodness bestowed on man. They are:

1. *Iman* (belief).
2. *Wilayat* (saintship).
3. *Nubuwwat* (prophethood).
4. *Risalat* (messengership).

Knowledge is essential for saintship which is friendship with Allah; and it is not necessary for belief; for belief depends on information and does not require knowledge as to the whereabouts of Allah or His possibility, etc. Saints are the first class scholars of Oneness; for Allah never takes an ignorant person as His friend. This is a big question which the customary scholars have overlooked. A solution of this question will include all monotheists under one sky, whatever may be the path pursued by them.

(*Al-Futuhat,* Vol. 2, p. 52)

Prophethood is an office conferred by the Elevator of Positions and Master of the Throne on a man of good character and wholesome behaviour. Generally, minds approve of it and thoughts do not reject it; reason accepts it; and it suits purposes and removes evils. When a man gets this office, it is the Prophethood of Allah in an absolute sense.

Of those that get such an office from the Elevator of Positions and Master of the Throne, if one feels a call to be the Prophet and Representative of Allah and gets an revelation of His commands in his mind, he is the trustworthy Representative of Allah, and his prophethood is a prophethood with a religion.

Allah says: "And thus We revealed you (spiritually) of Our commands . . . Thus angels bring down revelation by His order on those He chooses among His creatures... The Trustworthy Spirit entered your mind so that you may be one of the Admonishers."

Admonition is always connected with prophethood with a code. As for prophethood in general, there is no limit to its variations. It does not belong to any particular time. It will always continue in this world and in the other one. This is a question which the people of our path have ignored. not know if they did it want only, or if Allah did not inform them of it. Or, it may be, that they have dealt with it and it has not reached us. Allah knows best what it is.

Abu al-Bidar al-Tamashaki of Baghdad reported to me of Shaikh Bashir from our leaders at Bab al-Azj that the *Imam* of the times, Abd al-Qadir, said: "Prophets were given the title and we are given what they were not given." As to his saying, "They were given the title," it means that we are prevented from using the appellation "Prophet" even if prophethood continues among great men. And as to his saying, "He gave us what they were not given," it means what Khidr said to Moses. Allah proved the superiority and judgment of Khidr and humbled Moses, the Speaker with Allah, His chosen and intimate, on the point of certain knowledge.

Scholars know that Moses is superior to Khidr; but he said to Moses: "O Moses, I know that which Allah has taught me and which you do not know."

This is the exact meaning of 'Abd al Qadir's statement, when he said: "We are given what they were not given." If he had explicitly said, that by Prophets, he meant ordinary prophets, it would have been still more clear. For verily, Allah granted him what He did not grant to them. Allah has made the Prophets excel and be excelled. Such a thing cannot be denied.

(*Al-Futuhat,* Vol. 2, pp. 90-91)

Prophethood will continue till the Day of Resurrection in the world. Providing a code is but one function of prophethood. It is impossible that the information from Allah and the knowledge of His Universe should discontinue. If it discontinues, it will not be possible for the Universe to get food for its existence and continuance.

"Say, if the ocean were ink for the words of Allah, it would exhaust before the words of Allah exhausted, should We seek help from things, of its kind."

If all the trees were to be pens and all the oceans, were to be ink, the words of Allah could not be exhausted. Allah has informed that there is not a single thing which was created without the word "Be". These words of Allah never discontinue. They are the sustenance for the Universe and all existence. If providing a code, which is but one aspect of prophethood, ends, where are the other aspects?

(*Al-Futuhat,* Vol. 2, p. 90)

Myself and those that follow me are scholars about Allah, and are among those people of Allah whom Allah has appointed in the place of His Messengers in summoning men towards Him with the tongue of reality in virtue of the abstract prophethood which we hold of them in the matter of expounding truth—not prophethood with a code, but prophethood to protect the rule of the code through the insight of a protector and not through blind following. Prophethood with a code is quite different from prophethood in the absolute sense. He who has an absolute prophethood occupies the second grade, and he who has a code occupies the third. Prophets with new shari'at are called messengers. They have a code and a large following.

Their commands from Allah are what the natural forces inform them of. A prophet with a code is not in possession of complete knowledge as is seen from the behaviour of Moses, a prophet with a code, with Khidr, a prophet and friend of Allah.

(*Al-Futuhat,* Vol. 2, p. 52).

Nubuwwat is information to souls,
Confined by bodies having souls;
Whate'er's thus got is incomplete;
Only codes render it replete.
Often it is tidings with codes;
Now bliss forecasts, now woe forebodes.

(*Al-Futuhat,* Vol. 2, p. 254)

Know that prophethood of man is of two kinds. The first kind is from Allah to man without an angelic spirit between him and Allah. This office gives him Divine information which he finds in his own self from the hidden source or through revelations. These informations do not include allowance or prohibition but only impart Divine knowledge or knowledge about the truth of the code rules.

The second kind of human prophethood is of men who can be called the disciples of angels. The trustworthy spirit comes with a code, in their opinion, from Allah. He allows whatever he likes and forbids what ever he dislikes. These things took place before the days of Muhalnmad. Today there is no value to such revelations. It is the function of the *Mujtahidin*.

(*Al-Futuhat al-Makkiyyah,* Vol. 2, pp. 254-55).

As the Creator in the Irjun says,
It is in mind that He order lays.
They are the Prophets the chosen ones;
Verily, they are the common ones.
The grade of every angel is known.
As to the naked eye a hill is known.
One with another vies in nearness;
Some in speech have conciseness.

(*Al-Futuhat,* Vol. 2, p. 255)

When a man of illumination sees a figure which gives instructions in matters that he did not know before, that figure is from his own self proper. It is just like the figure in the mirror, which appears oblong or round, long or short, according to the character of the mirror.

(Al-Fasl-Shethiy-yah)

Angels are the powers hidden in the faculties and organs of man. *(Al-Fasl-Adamiyyah)*

By means of imagination, man creates forms that do not exist in the outer world. And the will-power guards the existence of these forms, and they are never exhausted. If a knower becomes inattentive to them, the forms disappear of themselves.

(Al-Fasl Ishaqiyyah).

The angel came to the Prophet in the world of thought. He saw him and recognised him as Gabriel with the eye of discernment. *(Al-Fasl Yusufiyyah)*

Prophethood and messengership are particular gifts from Allah, that is, there is no room for acquisition by man. These are mere gifts which are not given for any work, and for which Allah does not require gratitude. "Truly, We gave greatness to David of Ourselves"; and Allah did not require anything in exchange for this.

(Al-Fasl Dawudiyyah)

Know that saintship is a common and vast circle and its rule is that Allah chooses whomsoever He pleases of His creatures; and the rule of prophethood is that Allah chooses someone for messengership which is one of the functions of saintship. Every messenger must be a prophet and every Prophet must be a saint. Thus every messenger must be a saint and it is a special grade of saintship.

According to Abu al-Qa"sim, son of Qusai some of the messengers do not possess what the others

possess. Every one of them excels and is excelled.
(*Al-Futuhat* Vol. 2, pp. 256-57)

Verily, messengers are the tongue of reality for man, ordering, forbidding, informing and teaching. They are very intelligent men but that intelligence does not lead them to pride. Don't you hear them say what has been said regarding injuring the date trees ? They are of sound mind when they order as to permission or prohibition for men.

The worldly messengership has ended in our time, in accordance with what has been stated in the Message. But its function continues both in this world and the world to come. It has no bearing in existence proper. If there had been difficulties, the possessor of inspiration and messengership would not have spoken of inspiration and insight in others. The bee will be inspired always till Resurrection in its dwelling and among fruits.

Messengership is an intermediary state between the Sender and tl It is this state that is called messengership. It is not an absolute situation but only a relative one and ceases to exist the moment the Message is delivered. Allah says: "The Messenger has but to deliver." This is incumbent on him. He further says: "O Messenger, deliver what is sent unto you from your Lord." If you do not do it, you have n delivered His Message.

The Message, here, is what he is sent with and what he delivers. It occurs like this in the Qur'an wherever it occurs. The messenger does not take the Message except through a "Trustworthy Holy Spirit" who gets down into his mind with the Message. Sometimes the angel takes the form of a man. Inspiration not of the above description is not called a "Message". It is called inspiration, intuition, inclination, suggestion, or bubbling up. The difference between a prophet and a messenger is that the former gets an injunction for his own self which he must not convey to others and the latter gets an injunction to be conveyed to others— either to a particular group as in the case of all other messengers, or to all the nations as in the case of Muhammad (PBUH). None of the messengers before Muhammad (PBUH) can be called a messenger in this sense.

Every messenger is a prophet, but not is every prophet a messenger. The representatives are those who are ordered to deliver messages, such as, Ma'adb, Ali and Dahyat who were the messengers of the Messenger of Allah. Every one of the followers who is ordered to deliver a message in continuation of the message of the Messenger of Allah—from agent to agent—will be named a messenger. But this is not the messengership that has ended. The message that has ceased is the coming down of the Divine command through the agency of an angel in the particular form which we have pointed out above. This door is closed; but message without a code is not barred; nor is the Divine imparting in specific ways discontinued. And thus, the Qur'an came down into the minds of the saints. It did not cease in spite of the fact that it was protected and reserved. Some of the saints have an aptitude for inspiration.

It is due to this, that it is said of Abu Zaid that he did not die till he took the whole of the Qur'an through his back, that is, till he got it through inspiration. He is the person of whom the Prophet said: "The Qur'an is lodged between his sides." He did not say that he got it by heart. The meaning of taking through the back is getting through inspiration.

He got it as it continues among such of Allah's creatures as Allah likes. Besides, to this effect there is the saying of Allah: "The spirit is infused by His command in whom Allah likes among His creatures." The saints are capable of the prophethood of information and are not capable of the prophetho a code.

(*Al-Futuhat,* Vol. 2, pp. 258-59)

Verily messengership is bestowed. The recipient of this bounty need not desire it. He is born just, wise, knowing and comprehending. Neither knowledge nor action not holiness is condition precedent to it; but custom sees a prophet inclined towards good and in pleasant moods. (*Al-Futuhat*, Vol. 2, p. 256)

Between *Wilayat* and *Risalat* a *Barzakh* lies.
There the not unknown *Nubuwwat* lies.
That, again, is of two clear kinds;
One with code which the common praise,
The second is codeless and below
With the common, folk; but, for us,
The other does suit which is below.
Existence, its order, code destroys;
There, the other's beauty dawns.
Wider more and root is that:
On perfect saints knowledge dawns.

Muhammad (PBUH) said: "Prophethood and Messengership are cut off."

They were not cut off except in one particular respect. Only the appellations of "Prophet" and "Messenger" were cut off. It is on account of this that the Prophet said: "There is neither Prophet nor Messenger after me."

But there continue to be informers *(mubashshirin)* and law-givers (*mujtahidin)*. Only the names were dropped from them but the offices continue'. Those that are ignorant of the Divine precepts have to ask of these people, so that they may direct them in accordance with the result of their research. If they differ, they differ as religions and codes differ. "For every one of you, We have marked a code and a path."

Thus every *mujtahid* has made a code for himself in accordance with his own proof. His path is his chief proof for a particular injunction; and transgressing it is forbidden for him. Thus every one of them made a code in such a way that the *Shafa'i* forbade the very thing which the *Hanafi* permitted; and Abù Hanifa prohibited what Ahmed bin Hambal permitted. One allowed the very thing which another forbade. They gave their opinions of many things, and differed in many things. From every one of these there is a code for us from Allah. Yet we know that the position of these people was not that of the inspired messengers of Allah. Prophethood and messengership were not cut off in their essentials. But only the inspiration peculiar to a messenger or a prophet through an angel by His command was cut off.

(*Al-Futuhat,* Vol. 2, pp. 252-53)

Prophethood is to be found in animals. Allah says: "We sent message to the bee." Moreover it is to be found in all existence which the people of *Kashf* (gnosis) know.

(*Al-Futuhat al-Makkiyyah,* Vol. 2, p. 254)

CHAPTER X

ON REVELATION *(WAHI)*

Inspiration is the getting down of bare intelligible ideas into the confined organs of perception in the presence of thought, either in sleep or in the waking state. It is perceivable when the perceived is present. Allah said: "The Holy Spirit appeared to her (Mary) in the form of a complete man."

Ayisha (Allah be pleased with her) said: "The beginning of inspiration, in the case of Muhammad (PBUH), was in dreams. Whenever he dreamed, the dream dawned on him like the dawning of the morn." This, Allah has made permanent for all Muslims. It is a part of prophethood. Prophethood was not taken off completely. That is why we say the prophethood with code alone was taken off. This is the meaning of "There is no Prophet after me."

By saying that there is no prophet after Muhammad (PBUH), it is meant that there will be no Prophet with a code in particular. It is like saying:

"There will be no Kisra when Kisra perishes and there will be no Qaiser when Qaiser perishes." There is no Kisra" except in Persia and no Qaiser except in Rome. The Roman emperor still continues; but the name Qaiser has ceased, although there is an emperor among the Romans. We call the emperors of Persia and Rome by other names, after the death of Kisra and Qaiser.

Similarly, the name of Prophet ceased after Muhammad (PBUH): for the coming in of new code from Allah through inspiration has ceassd after him. None has formulated a code after him except in the matter of judging with the insight of a law giver. This is done by scholars in virtue of the appointment by the Messenger of Allah which is valid. The *mujtahid* has to give orders in accordance with the orders of Allah already given to the Prophet. He cannot approve of matters not approved by Allah. It is a matter known to Muslims and saints that Muhammad (PBUH) was endowed with the most perfect accomplishments in all matters. So he was perfect in the matter of inspiration also. That is, be had all kinds and sorts of inspiration. Muhammad (PBUH) says: "I was given all languages and was sent among all mankind." There was not a single sort of inspiration which he did not receive. In accordance with this view, his inspiration began with dream for six months. We are taught that the beginning of inspiration is dream. It is not necessary that every Prophet should begin with dreams. It may be by some other means. When Muhammad (PBUH) began it with dream, we can certainly say that dream is the beginning of inspiration. Muhammad being the most perfect of the inspired, the beginning of his inspiration should be the beginning of inspiration itself.

Therefore, in our opinion, inspiration begins with senses and then evolves towards supersensual matters. The inspiration mentioned above is regarding codes of religions through prophets and messengers but not in an absolute sense.

As regards inspiration pure and simple,, or inspiration amongst the various kinds of objects inspired, like angels and non-human animal species, it is as Allah says, "Allah inspired the bee." As regards in animate objects, it is as in the case of offering the *Amanat* to the, skies and the earth and the mountains; for the offer was through inspiration; and also as in the following verses: "He inspired unto all the skies regarding His order ... He inspired the wicked among them and the pious."

Inspiration is common to all—man, *jinn,* the wicked and the pious. "These are all the blessings of Allah; and the blessings of Allah are not limited."

(*At-Futuhat,* V61. 2, p. 58)

Wahi is that which gives a sign which does the function of an expression. From an expression, it is possible to understand the meaning intended by it; and it is on this account, that it is called an expression as opposed to the sign which is *Wahi*. It is the essence of the directed himself, that directs. *Wahi* is the first understood, the first understanding: there is nothing more quick than one being the essence of understanding, the essence of making one understand and the essence of the understood. If you do not understand this you are not an inspired man. Do you not see that inspiration is rapidity and that there can be nothing more rapid than what we have mentioned ? This kind of speech is called inspiration when it is in this fashion, that is, it is a reflection of my own essence.

Therefore, it is said in the Information that when Allah speaks through inspiration it is like a chain on a stone struck by the angels. *Wahi* is the language of reality, which very quickly affects the mind of the hearer. This is not known except to knowers through Divine tokens; for it is the essence of Divine inspiration in the Universe.

Often *Wahi* is Divine perception through faith. Everything is created with this capacity and there is no need for any training in *Wahi*. A new born child finds out the breasts of its mother. This is an effect of Divine *Wahi* which is sent to it as He says: "We are nearer to it than you are; but you do not see," and He further says: "Your Allah sent *Wahi* to the bee to construct houses (Honey-combs) on hills, trees and elevated places." If the bee had not understood the inspiration of Allah it would not have obeyed him in the light of His commands. Therefore, if a speech is a *Wahi* its contradiction cannot be imagined; for its force is too strong to be resisted.

Allah says: "We inspired the mother of Moses, 'Suckle him and when thou fearest for him, throw him into the river'." She did accordingly and did not contradict although she was commanded to throw Moses into destruction. She did not contradict, nor did she hesitate; nor did human judgment overcome her that throwing her child into the river in a box was the most dangerous thing.

This proves that inspiration is more powerful in the mind of the inspired than his nature.

Allah says: "We are nearer to him than the jugular vein." The jugular vein is in his person itself.

So, Saints, if you think that Allah has inspired you, look into your mind, as to the possibility of hesitation or contradiction; if you find any, through one effort, analysis or meditation, you are not inspired. If it overpowers you, blinds you, deafens you and shuts your thoughts and efforts and its order operates on you automatically, it is inspiration; and you are, in that case, a man of inspiration.

CHAPTER XI

ON LOVE AND TOLERATION

The constitution of man may be divided into three items:

1. Soul.
2. Body.
3. Self.

Allah made the form (in essence) of man, in His own form; and no one could unravel the mystery of man's formation except Allah Himself. One who wishes to destroy that formation beyond the limits of law, becomes an aggressor over his own self. He wishes to destroy that which Allah wishes to habilitate. To treat Allah's creatures with kindness and to safeguard them are better than enforcing His law with severity.

When David wanted to construct the holy house at Jerusalem, he tried at it several times. The house used to collapse every time that it was raised. He complained about it to Allah, when a revelation came to him: "Verily, My house will not stand at the hands of one who has spilled blood" David said: "My Lord, was not this blood spilling in Thy way ?" The reply was: "Yes, it was in My way, but were they not My creatures ?" Then David prayed: "O Lord, make it at the hands of one who will be in my progeny." Then the revelation came that his son Solomon would do it.

This story is cited to show that leniency towards Allah's creatures is far better than enforcing the severity of law. This is why it becomes incumbent to make peace with the enemies of religion and to simply levy Jaziah, so that they are not exterminated. If they are inclined towards peace, you shall also become inclined towards it. In the case of murder, blood-money is to be accepted, if the heirs of the murdered person agree to it. If there are several heirs, the opinion of one who agrees is to be given preference over the opinions of those who are recalcitrant. A person was killed by the lashing of a camel's leather-strap; the Prophet let go the accused as a leather-strap was not a thing intended for killing.

Allah has said: "Retribution of evil is evil commensurate with it." Retribution, although sanctioned by the law, is still an evil. Allah rewards those who give it up and tender pardon in exchange for blood-money; for the murderer is in the image of Allah. Pardon is thus received by One who forms the image of the murderer, and therefore, Allah rewards the pardoner.

The name of Allah, "the Apparent, became manifest from the existence of the creature and he who respects Him respects this name. Man is not blameworthy in respect of his reality, but is blameworthy in respect of his action which is not his reality. Action does not proceed from anybody except Allah. Allah has the preservation of the life of the creatures always in view. You should have the same in view, for by preserving life, you reach that acme of perfection for which Allah has intended you. Instead of killing one another, you should resort to the con-templation of Allah, *(Al-Fasl Dawudiyyah)*

Allah is never seen immaterially; and the vision of Him in woman is the most perfect of all.

(Fusus al-Hikam, p. 245)

Love is the highest form in which Allah is worshipped. (*Fusus al-Hikam,p.* 245)

Do you know that Allah's commands require harmony and order ? *(Al-Fasl IshB-qiyyah)*

My heart is capable of every form; A cloister for the monk, a fane for idols, A pasture for gazelles, the votary's Ka'bah. The tables of the Torah and the Qur'an.

Love is the creed I hold.
Wherever turn His camels,
Love is still my creed and faith.

(Ibne 'Arabi, quoted in *Nafh ut-Tib)*

www.ingramcontent.com/pod-product-compliance
Lightning Source LLC
Chambersburg PA
CBHW062144160726
48282CB00027B/932
* 9 7 8 9 3 9 0 8 0 4 7 7 1 *